Being Set Free
from
Family Secrets

SHAWNETTA BROWN

Copyright © 2018 Shawnetta Brown
All rights reserved
First Edition

PAGE PUBLISHING, INC.
New York, NY

First originally published by Page Publishing, Inc. 2018

Due to the graphic and vulgar depictions described, this book is for mature audiences only.

ISBN 978-1-64350-753-8 (Paperback)
ISBN 978-1-64350-754-5 (Digital)

Printed in the United States of America

I dedicate this book to God; my daughter, Talayia Reed; and my son, Deshawn Bessix.

I would like to thank my pastor, of Seeds of Greatness Bible Church, Pastor Jerome, and First Lady Sis Lisa Lewis for being strong leaders and teaching me to stay inspired and to always remember "*My faith is not fragile, my faith is not weak, my faith gets stronger every time I speak!*"

For "Everyone who calls on the name of the Lord will be saved."

—Romans 10:13

INTRODUCTION

Hello, reader, my name is Shawnetta Brown, my nickname is Dee, and I wanted to first take a moment to thank you for your support and your readership. I'll confess in advance, I am not a writer. I've never really had the desire to write a book, but when the seed was planted that I should share my story and testimony, God led me to this book. Over the past two decades, I have made it my mission to dedicate my life over to God as a living sacrifice. A part of that mission has required me to share my story with others who felt as though God couldn't help them. One of my favorite places to share my story is the women's prison and shelters. It's been in these places that I've met so many women who were just like me, lost, broken, and hurt. I use my life to show them change can happen at any point in your life.

One of my goals for this book is to create a space where people of different ethnicity of all cultures and, community, can have conversations about family secrets. Growing up, my family didn't talk much about the hardships we faced, and as children, we were to be "seen and not heard." As a result, we lived double lives: there was the life we actually lived and the life we portrayed. My family did a great job of keeping their secrets untold—including me.

Let me share a little more background about myself. Please understand, this is the life that I lived. It was crazy and unthinkable. You will see that I really didn't have much of a choice in most of my decisions as a young child or teenager. Once I became old enough to realize what happened to me throughout my childhood into my young adult life, I began to also realize the negative effect those incidents had on my life in the future. You see, I am a people person. I love seeing people happy, and I like making people happy, whether it be with a smile, a hug, or whatever. I didn't get that affection as a child or young adult; I guess you could say *I was looking for love in all the wrong places.*

As God prepared me to tell this story, I struggled with Him, back and forth telling Him, "I would love to tell my story, but, God, I don't want people judging me and looking at me sideways because of the life I led." That was when God told me, "It's not about you, it's about everyone else who has gone through this or may go through something similar to your story." So I prayed and asked God to help me with my story, and He did just that.

As you read this story, I want you to take a moment and place yourself in my shoes. Some of the material is graphic and/or vulgar. But it is real. This is a true account of my life. I have changed the names of family and friends used in the story to protect those involved in my life's identity. This book is for mature audiences only.

Please enjoy my testimony, and I pray that you are led to have a conversation with your family and friends about the hardships of life. We can no longer keep secrets at the risk of those we love.

CHAPTER 1

Tragedy That Changed My Destiny

Hello, my name is Shawnetta Brown, nickname Dee. I was born on March 17, 1967, to my mom, Cheryl, and my father, Andre. Shortly after my birth, my parents were married, and a year later, my mom gave birth to my little brother, Edward. My mother was a pretty good mom. She was not very affectionate, but she made sure my brother and I had everything we needed. She was of that old-school generation where the man dictated how things should be. Although she was pretty bubbly, you never really heard her speak up very often. She was also very hardworking. I can remember times during my childhood when she worked three jobs at a time.

As for my father, from what I can remember, he was an Army man and had served in the Vietnam War. Once he came home, my mom told my brother and me that Daddy had been through some bad ordeals and experiences while away at war, but she never elaborated on what those experiences were. I can remember how my father would drift off and daydream while driving us to our aunt's house in Maryland.

One night, in October of 1971, my father, along with four of his friends, went out to make a run to the local liquor store. That run turned into the last time I'd ever see my father alive. On their way back to the house, they were involved in a tragically fatal car accident claiming all their lives, including the other driver that they hit head-on. I can remember that night as if it were yesterday. I was only four years old. I can remember someone knocking at the door and saying only a few words before my mom started screaming and crying. In a confused state, she scrambled to get me and my brother together to go with her and the person who came to tell her that her husband had been in a bad car accident. We went to the accident site, and I remember seeing the bright flashing lights from the ambulance and police cars lighting up the sky. As a four-year-old, it was hard to comprehend the death of my father in that moment with all the excitement of lights and officials running around. I do not remember much else after that night.

A couple years following the death of my father, when I was around six years old and my brother, Edward, was about five years old, our mom started dating this guy named Rick. Rick was a short dark-skinned man with short wavy hair. There was something about him that I didn't understand—he had this very suspicious vibe about him. It wasn't long after they started dating before my mom told me and Ed that she was getting married to Mr. Suspicious. Before they actually married, my mom would take Ed and me to our deceased father's parents' house, while she and Rick went out for nights on the town.

From what I can remember, I had three uncles that lived with my grandparents. I didn't like going over to my grandparents' house because that meant we had to go into the dungeon. The dungeon was the room located in the very back of the house. It was an add-on and was very dark, with limited lighting, an old TV, and paneled walls. The family used that room as the sitting room, but because you couldn't see into the room from anywhere else and could easily hear if someone was coming, it was used for more than just "sitting."

When my mom took my brother and me over to my grandparents' home, it was typically one of my uncles watching us, and every time we were there, one of our uncles would sexually molest me and my brother, Ed. I don't know if they knew what the other was doing or if it was just a coincidence that whoever babysat us had their "time." They would make us perform oral sex on them. Little did we know that we were being used as sex pawns and that it was wrong, disgusting, and sick. This went on for a couple of years, 1973–1975. They told us to never tell anyone, that it was our *secret*. As my brother and I grew up, we didn't discuss or tell anyone the terrible things that were done to us as small children. Although we didn't talk about it, the memory of what they would do to us haunted me as I grew. It wasn't until I became older that I began to understand what they did to us was a violation of our rights as a human being and in the eyes of God—they robbed us of our innocence.

A few years later, I was about twelve and Ed was around eleven, and the seed of life was planted in my world. My uncle Willie, my dad's oldest brother, came home for a family visit. Uncle Willie was not like our other uncles; instead, Uncle Willie made a great career for himself and his family. In fact, in 1969, at the age of twenty-six, he was the first African American to become a state police trooper in Delaware. He moved on to become part of the FBI in Chicago, Illinois. During his visit, he pulled my brother and me to the side and asked if we believed in Jesus Christ. We told him, "Yes." He then asked us if we would like to receive Jesus as our Lord and Savior. He had us read Romans 10:8–10. I'll never forget that day because it was obvious my uncle Willie was a Christian and actually took time out to sit with us and teach us a little bit about God—something we hadn't experienced from a family member before. While that was the first seed of life, it would be a long time before I began to see any good fruit grow into my life.

CHAPTER 2

How the Secrets Got Started: Mama Married the Wrong Man

As I transitioned into my teenage years, I believed that in order to make a boy or a man happy, I was to please him in *every* way that I could. I became a very passive, naive, and promiscuous young woman. I lost my virginity at age fourteen. My destiny was about to change.

It was at this tender age of fourteen years old when I thought things were finally looking bright for my future. I just acquired my first job at Gino's, and I was really excited! One weekend, I went to stay with my grandparents in Maryland (this was my mom's dad and her stepmother).

While she was my mom's stepmother, I still referred to her as Mom-mom. Her nephew Jack, from Philadelphia, Pennsylvania, was also visiting for the weekend. Now keep in mind, Jack was not biologically related to me. We were cousins only through marriage. One day, during our visit, Jack and I were on the couch watching TV. Jack was sitting up, and I was lying down, with my head on his lap, and my grandparents were out shopping. When they came back and saw me lying in his lap, my grandmother started yelling and arguing with me, saying that Jack and I were being "nasty" with each other. The truth of the matter was, we weren't; we were just watching TV. The next day she called my mom to come pick me up. When my mom arrived and asked what happened, I tried explaining to her that we did nothing wrong. I pleaded with her that "Mom-mom just assumed we were being nasty." Without really acknowledging what happened, she simply told me, "Gather your things and we will just go." We didn't really talk much on our ride home. I take it she was upset or maybe confused. When we finally arrived, I remember my mom walking in the house and immediately telling my stepfather, Rick, what happened.

The next day, a Sunday, my mom went to work (she often worked the weekend shifts). Once my mom was gone, Rick came into my bedroom, woke me up, and said, "Your mom wants me to talk to you about what had happened at your grandparents' house." Not really thinking much of it, I got up and went into their bedroom as I was instructed. Slightly annoyed at being woken out of my sleep, I told him the same story I told my mom. In my head, all I could think was, *Why is he waking me up to talk about this now, why not wait until I got up?* Rick kept asking the same questions. Still half asleep and frustrated, I sarcastically said to him, "*No!* I did not have sex with Jack." The next thing I know, Rick was pushing me down on the bed, aggressively touching me on my breast and my vagina, saying, "Don't say a word!" I didn't know what to do, and my sister and brothers were still sleeping. Rick *raped* me! I was in total shock and terrified all at the same time. When he finished, he told me to not tell my mother or anyone. He said, "If you want anything or to go anywhere with your friends, just let me know, and I'll make sure your mom lets you go." He proceeded to tell me to go back to my room, as if nothing happened. I was distraught! I couldn't believe that my stepfather just raped me and acted as if it were normal. I had all kinds of thoughts running through my mind. I started crying and asking myself why was this happening to me again, but this time, my perpetrator went all the way.

After a couple passing days, I started thinking, *Maybe this is my fault.* I *never* gave this man any indication that I liked/wanted him in any kind of way. When my mom started dating him, there was something about him I didn't like, but I didn't understand what it was. I was between the age of six or seven when he married my mom, and I finally knew why I was having those ill feelings toward him.

About a week later, my stepfather tried to come in my bedroom to rape me again. This time, more alert, I immediately jumped up out of my bed and yelled for him to get out before I called Edward. He left my room that day unaccomplished. This moment left me feeling debilitated. All I could think was, *Is he going to keep coming back in here and try and rape me again?* Well, I didn't want that, but I was too scared to say anything! I used to see this stuff on the news about children being sexually abused by their parents. I couldn't believe that this was actually happening to me.

Uncertain of what to do, I decided to tell Ed what had happened to me. After telling him this, he was very mad. He said, "We have to tell Mom."

I argued and begged with him, "No, because he will hurt me." Ed said, "I don't care what you say. I'm telling Mom."

You see, Ed wanted to tell because we didn't tell when we were younger about our uncles molesting us. *Not this time.*

So later that day, Ed told Mom, and she asked me, "Is it true?"

With tears in my eyes, I told her, "Yes, and that he promised if I allowed him to be with me that he would allow me to go out with my friends, even if you said no—"

Before I could finish, my mom said very sternly to me, "I don't want to hear any more of this." Therefore, I shut my mouth.

After about a day or so, I went to my mom thinking we could talk about it more and said to her, "Oh yeah … Mom, Rick told me if I didn't say anything to you that I would be allowed to hang out with my friends more."

Well, she shut me down and screamed, "I don't want to hear any more about this! Your dad told me everything that happened."

Confused, I said, "What are you talking about, Mom?"

She continued, "He told me how you were throwing yourself at him and that you wanted him."

I looked at her with such disgust and anger in my eyes and said, "Mom, I never wanted your husband, and I have no reason to lie to you."

She didn't want to hear anything I had to say. She told me I better *not* tell one person about this. "I mean it."

That was that. I then realized my mom married the wrong man.

As I walked away from her, I started crying because my mom chose her husband over me. I can't begin to explain how hurt and upset I was. I started to feel like it was my fault again, that my mom blamed me and, what's worse, didn't *love* me anymore. Here I was, this fourteen-year-old girl who, up until this point, loved life and her mom very much, but as I went through the rest of middle and high school, I no longer felt my mother's love.

I carried this secret from 1980 until I became an adult and only shared it with my two best friends. I lived in the home with my stepfather and mother, but I was only physically there. The family unit didn't exist for me after that.

Now, to backtrack a little, if you recall, I stated earlier that I was fourteen years old when I lost my virginity. This happened prior to being raped. I lost it to a young man who lived in my neighborhood, named Vincent. He and I had sex, but we didn't really do much after that.

Moving forward in time a little, when I turned fifteen, I started working at McDonald's. Vincent was nineteen years old, and as many young girls experience with older boys, I had a huge crush on him. However, even with my crush, it wasn't until I was seventeen going on eighteen years old that I asked my mom if I could date Vincent. Laughing, she said, "You might as well … since you have been sneaking around with him for a couple of years now."

Surprised, I said to her, "How did you know Mom?"

Still laughing, she simply replied, "Moms know everything."

Vincent and I started dating in 1984. After graduating from high school, I wanted to go to the community college for business administration, in Dover, Delaware. I figured this would be a good field considering I liked doing office work and organizing things. I registered myself, and I started going to Del-Tech Community College in September 1985.

I am sad to say I only completed one semester, and that was to complete my prerequisites. I decided I wanted to work full time at McDonald's and that I'd go to school later.

My brother, Ed, graduated the year after me, in 1986, and decided to enlist in the Navy. He served four years and even served in Desert Strom. I was hoping that this could somehow bring some good into Ed's life and help him recover from all the bad that had happened to us. I really just wanted him to find some peace and forgiveness in his heart to let go of our past.

I should have finished college when I started; this turned out to be one of my major mistakes in my life. But you know when you're young and lack guidance, you tend to want to do everything your own way.

After dating Vincent for a year, he proposed to me on Christmas day 1986, and of course, I said *yes*! He gave me an absolutely beautiful ring, and I felt like I was on top of the world.

Chapter 3

When the Unexpected Happens

In January of 1987, I was nineteen years old going on twenty years old. I started looking for a new job, a higher-paying job, to be exact; therefore, I applied for a job that was about an hour drive from my house to New Castle, with Curtis Industries. My neighbor, a girl named Bobbi Joe, was already working there. Shortly after submitting my application, I received a call to come in for an interview. I eagerly obliged and went in a few days later for my interview. The interview went well and I got the job. Bobbi Joe and I decided to carpool each week; that helped us both save on gas and limit the wear and tear on our cars. I was best friends with Bobbi Joe's sister, Lynn. We grew up together and hung out almost every day when we were teenagers.

At this point, I was at a stage in my life where I smoked marijuana and socially drank, but I had nothing to do with heavy drugs. After about three months of working at the factory, I met this guy named Jonathan. He was just hired that spring of 1987. They also hired his sister, Linda, and his friend, Mark.

Jonathan seemed like he was a nice guy. I had to train him some days on how to pick orders, so naturally we started talking more frequently. As time went on, Jonathan and I started liking each other. I told him I was in a relationship and that I had been engaged for about five months. He was like, "Oh, okay." I asked him if he was in a relationship, and he told me he wasn't, and in fact, he only had a few friends that he kicked it with. He did, however, tell me that he had a baby on the way by this younger girl but that it was just a thing, not a relationship.

I started hanging out with Jonathan and Linda during our lunch breaks almost daily. I enjoyed hanging out with them; they were funny, decent people. After a few weeks of us hanging out during lunch, Jonathan asked me to come and hang out with him and some of his friends that Saturday. I didn't see anything wrong with it, so I called my girlfriend Tiff that Saturday morning and asked if she would like to hang out with me and this guy that I met at my job. Tiff was one of my best friends, my partner in crime. Tiff was about my height, five feet, five inches, chocolate-colored skin, very pretty, with natural curly hair, and average build. She had a one-year-old daughter, whom I loved dearly, as if she were my own. Tiff said, "Sure, I'm not doing anything today. It's Saturday, why not." Before we confirmed our plans, Tiff said, "Wait a minute, what about Vincent?"

I knew it was wrong, but I said, "I know! But I'm not going to do anything with him, I just want to go and hang out with his sister and a couple of his friends."

Hesitantly Tiff agreed, so I drove to pick her up, and we headed up to the city where Jonathan lived. Tiff and I were country girls. We were raised in the country with the animals, birds, snakes, etc., and we were okay with it. I was glad to have been raised in the country. Everyone felt like family where we lived.

Once we were in the city, I met up with Johnathan, and he went to get some drinks and some weed to smoke. After hanging for a while, Jonathan asked me to pick up one of his friends, Robin. He seemed to be a cool guy. He was kind of dark skinned, with pretty eyes and a nice stature. After picking up Robin, Jonathan wanted to go get more drinks and something to eat. After making all our runs, we all ended up back at Robin's house.

We were sitting around, drinking, talking, and smoking a little bit of weed, getting to know one another.

With no warning, Jonathan pulled out this bag of cocaine, and he and Robin began talking about "cooking up" something with each other. At this point, Tiff and I didn't know what was going on.

Neither of us were familiar with drug usage, but we didn't want to make a big deal out of what was happening around us.

Next, Jonathan took out this test tube and put the cocaine in it, along with some water and something else, a white powder substance. At that time we didn't know what it was, but it turned out to be baking soda.

Like a child seeing something foreign yet intriguing for the first time, I asked Jonathan, "What in the hell is that?"

Nonchalantly he said to me, "We're cooking up cocaine, which turns into *rock*."

Still intrigued, I continued to ask, "Okay, and then what do you do with it?"

He said, "You smoke it."

I said, "*Oh*. Well, I have never seen this before, nor have I ever heard of it."

Jonathan explained, "Not many people do it because the cocaine is expensive, it's not cheap." He then said, "You don't have to try it if you don't want to."

Relieved a bit, I said to him, "Good, I'm okay … Tiff and I will just smoke our weed and drink our coolers."

The following weekend, Tiff and I decided to go back into the city and hang out again with Jonathan and his boy Robin. We had a repeat of last weekend. I asked Jonathan to get me and Tiff some weed and some coolers to drink, so he did. And just like last weekend, Jonathan and Robin decided they were going to cook up some cocaine and smoke it.

Jonathan asked me and Tiff if we wanted to try some of the coke. This time, Tiff and I looked at each other and said, "Okay, why not?" so Tiff and I took a pull off the glass pipe, which was a small glass bowl that had a tiny little bowl at the top of it in which you put the cooked cocaine in. You then added fire to the rock. As the rock melted, you pulled the smoke from the melted rocks from a stem that extended from the bowl, the part you put your lips on.

I decided to go first. I did exactly what Jonathan told me to do, but I didn't feel any change, so Tiff decided to take her turn, and she repeated the same steps I took. Still no change. So Jonathan said, "It's probably because it's your first time doing it." Therefore, we waited a few minutes and repeated those same steps again. This time we got the *full effect*! My eyes instantly got wider, and I felt like I had to keep moving around, doing things, like cleaning, talking, anything. It was like being uncontrollably *hyper* and fidgety. I was like "*Wow! What is going on?*" Tiff went next, and she felt it this time as well and received the same effect I did.

That evening we kept on smoking the cocaine with Jonathan and Robin. Little did we know that this drug was going to change our lives forever—this was when the unexpected happened.

CHAPTER 4

Going Nowhere, Part 1

As Jonathan and I continued to work at the same company, we also continued seeing each other outside the job. We would get off work on Fridays and went to Philly to buy cocaine. By this point, I started buying my own cocaine to smoke, right along with Jonathan and his friends.

To keep things going, I kind of lied to Vincent, my fiancé. I told him I met this girl on my job, and on Fridays, I would hang out with her at her place. It was true, *partially*. See, I kind of left out the part about how her brother had a crush on me and how I was mostly hanging out with him also.

This went on for a couple of months, and within that time, I realized that *I liked smoking cocaine*. Within those few months, I had sniffed cocaine before, but I never made it a habit. It was just sometimes. *Smoking* it was different. It was a different kind of high. Smoking it seemed to get you so high that you just wanted to stay there, in that moment.

I started to see Jonathan more and more behind my fiancé's back. I didn't like it because I wasn't a cheater, but I had never been so infatuated by another man before this, besides my fiancé.

Jonathan was a nice-looking man. He was about five feet, ten inches or so, brown skinned, dark-brown eyes, and a muscular body, like he worked out. He had just come home from the Navy a few months prior, so that helped explain his physique. Every time I saw him, I would say to myself, "Damn, he's so fine."

He always smelled so good, and I found myself wanting him and fantasizing about what it would be like to make love to him.

I was talking to Tiff about Jonathan, telling her how much I was starting to like him. I told Tiff that I was going to break off my engagement to Vincent.

One day I had to meet my fiancé at his aunt's house for a barbecue. When I arrived, I pulled him to the side, and I shared with him that I did not want to stay in the relationship and that I was breaking off the engagement. His reaction was similar to that of any generally hurt man, and of course, he wasn't feeling that, nor was he trying to hear it. He asked me why I was calling off the engagement. I told him I met someone and that I wanted to date him. We got into this big argument which escalated into him slapping me upside my head. Terrified, I ran to my car and left. That was the last time I ever talked to Vincent.

When I left the argument, I immediately went to pick Tiff up, and we headed back to the city, where Jonathan was. We hung out there with Jonathan and his friends the rest of the evening.

Every weekend after we got off work, Jonathan, Linda, Robin, and I would drive up to Philadelphia to *cop some coke* and head right back to Wilmington to cook it up and smoke it. Tiff and I were getting high every weekend with the crew. There were times Linda, Jonathan's sister, would come party with us, but most of the time she would be with her boyfriend.

Around this time, Tiff and I had just moved into our first apartments. I had a one-bedroom, and Tiff had a two-bedroom, for her and her daughter.

At this point, Tiff and I didn't see smoking cocaine as a problem. We looked at it as something to do and having fun with some guys we liked. For months, Tiff and I continued to hang out with Jonathan and friends, getting high. Progressively, I started to miss days from work from being up all night getting high. I started calling out sick more and more frequently. Tiff didn't have a job at this time. She was home raising her daughter. This went on the whole summer of 1987.

Well, as one would expect, I ended up losing my job and ultimately my apartment. I had nowhere to go. I called my cousin Candy and asked her to ask my aunt June if I could come stay with them until I could get back on my feet. I started to feel like I was going *nowhere*.

Knowing I needed to work, I began the search for employment and landed a job with this company called Sparks Industries in Dover, Delaware. I was a secretary, and I really enjoyed my job. After working there for a couple of months, my boss, Mr. White, started to flirt with me, asking me out on a date. Mr. White was about sixty-five years old. He was a short Italian man, with short gray hair, tanned skin, a big nose and huge stomach, but also a *big heart*! When I started there, I was only twenty-one years old. All I could think was, *Why in the world do you want to take me out? I'm too young*, laughing it off as if it was joke.

Somewhere around 1988, I had about four months in working with Mr. White. Up until that point, I thought everything was going well. He constantly commended me for my hard work, and I was consistent in getting my work completed on time. But one day, Mr. White came to me and said, "I'm so sorry, Shawnetta, but I am going to have to lay you off from work." Mr. White stated that his business had slowed down, and he couldn't afford to keep me on his payroll. Instantly, I became quiet and sad. I asked, "Okay, Mr. White, but if your business picks back up, will you call me back?" He cheerfully said, "Yes, I will." Which gave me some reassurance. I said thank you and proceeded to pack up my belongings. As I was packing up to leave, Mr. White proceeded to ask me, "Will it be okay for me to take you out to dinner?" This time, I said, "Sure, why not."

After about a week, Mr. White called to set up our dinner date. We agreed on the next day. At this time, I no longer had my car, it had been repossess and I was living with my aunt and cousin. The next day arrived, and Mr. White came over to my cousin Candy's house to pick me up. I felt more comfortable bringing Candy along, so I asked Mr. White, "Do you mind if my cousin Candy comes along with us?" Mr. White said, "Sure, I have no problem with that."

Being that I didn't know Mr. White very well, I felt I needed someone with me that I could trust.

As we were having dinner, very discreetly, Mr. White propositioned me, to see if I was interested in having sex with him, and he would pay me. *Hmmmmm ... well that was* bold *of him. Right to the point he went.* At this time, I' was thinking, *Well, I don't have a job, I could use the money.* I told him I needed to talk to my cousin about his offer and I'd let him know. He said, "Okay." After Mr. White dropped Candy and me off home, I told her what he had asked of me. Candy said, "Well, that is up to you. Did he say how much he will give you?" I told her he didn't say but that I'd find out.

The next day I was talking to Candy, and I said to her, I had *never* had anyone proposition me for sex *and pay me for it.* Candy said, "I know." Now knowing I liked to smoke cocaine and party, I had a new interest in the idea. Besides, *I could get* paid*!* I knew I was not a prostitute, and I wasn't trying to become one. *I just want what I want.* I told Candy that I was getting ready to call Mr. White back and ask him exactly what he wanted from me. That Friday, I called Mr. White, and I asked him, "What is it exactly that you want from me?"

Mr. White responded by saying, "You are beautiful, and I am very attracted to you, and I have never been attracted to a black woman before. I want to be able to help you and buy you things, like lingerie, so you can model it for me."

Flattered, I laughed at him and said, "You're something else. I thank you for the compliment."

He went on to say, "I'll pay you $200 to $300 if you come to my beach house once a week to see me, and we just have oral sex." He wanted to cook for me as well—he loved to cook.

He stated that I only had to stay a couple of hours at his home when I did come. I told Mr. White, the only way I'd do it was if my cousin Candy could come with me or one of my girlfriends; you see, I wasn't trying to be alone with him. Again Mr. White was very accommodating and said, "Sure, I have no problem with that."

Later on that evening, Mr. White came and picked me and Candy up and drove us to his beach house. Once we got there, he welcomed us into his home and told us to get comfortable. He poured us a glass of wine and put on some jazz music for us to listen to. He made some homemade bread and pasta for us for dinner—*it was delicious.*

After dinner, Mr. White and I stepped off into his bedroom, and I left Candy in the living room, relaxing. I went into the bathroom to change into the lingerie he had bought me. Mr. White asked me to model for him, so I did.

Now picture me, I'm five five, cocoa brown, built like an Amazon brick house, 34-26-36. He is staring at me like he just hit the Jackpot (internally, I struggled to maintain my composure and keep from laughing).

When I walked out, I was a little nervous, considering this was my first rodeo at this here game.

Mr. White had already taken off his clothes and was lying on the bed, waiting on me. I lay down beside him. He started touching me, rubbing his hands all over my body and kissing me on my breast. I kept rolling my eyes in my head, trying not to get sick, knowing I didn't want him touching me. He started to work himself down between my legs, kissing them, and then he started sucking my vagina. I started shaking and moving around because, while I didn't want him touching me, *it was feeling too darn good!* As we continued to do our business, I went down on him and pretended that I was giving him oral sex, when really, I was just licking it. I did *not* want to perform oral sex on him. In my mind, that was disgusting to me, and it brought back memories of when my uncles made me do it.

So I had an idea. Since his stomach was so big and his penis was small, I decided going forward that this was how I would get over on him. I would continue to play, *lick* on his penis, and get *paid!* How many girls do you know that can get paid to be pleasured?

Mr. White was so infatuated with me I don't think he really cared if we did or didn't have sex. He shared with me that he had a girlfriend, who was close to his age, but said he was not happy with their sex life.

After being at his house for about two hours, I asked Mr. White if he could take me and my cousin, Candy home. We got dressed, and he pulled out his checkbook and wrote me out a check for $300. I politely took my earnings, and he then took us back home to Dover.

After Mr. White dropped me and Candy off, we ran into the house and upstairs to Candy's room to discuss what just happened. All we could both do was laugh. I boasted, "Wow! That was the fastest $300 that I had ever made." And off to the drug dealer we went.

The following week approached, and this time, my best friend, Tiff, wanted to roll out with me and Mr. White. It was a Wednesday night, and Mr. White came over to pick me up, and then we headed straight to Tiff's dad's house to pick her up.

I had already let Tiff know what was going on with Mr. White. Tiff was always down with the get down. She was my ride-or-die, go-hard best friend! Plus, Tiff wanted to get some money, as well as myself. She asked me if I'd mind if she and Mr. White messed around too. Laughing, I said, "Hell no, I don't mind, he's not my man. I just want to get money to go get high." Tiff said, "You damn right!"

By the end of the night, I had a check for $200, and Tiff had a check for $150. Mr. White told me if I bring any of my girlfriends and they wanted to have some fun, he would pay them. But the best part about this arrangement was that I didn't always have to be the one he was with. He was cool as long as he was with a black woman. He said I'd still get a check just because he "loved" me. *Hahaha, sure, I thought.* It couldn't get any better than that. This went on for the rest of the summer of 1988, but Mr. White began to fade out of the picture. I guess he had either gotten his chocolate fix or his habit was becoming too costly.

Tiff and I started meeting other drug dealers that were selling cocaine locally. Before you knew it, Tiff and I were hanging out with men that were no good for or to us.

I still didn't have a job, and I was still living with Candy and Aunt June.

Tiff and I introduced smoking cocaine to her dad, Mr. Frank. That probably was one of the worst things we could have ever done. He was a paraplegic and *hell on wheels, hahaha*. Once he got started, he wanted to control everyone and everything associated with smoking cocaine. He would invite some of his friends over, and we would get high and stay up for days smoking coke.

The drug dealers would come to the house, and when we didn't have any more money, Tiff and I would turn tricks with them (have sex with them) so we could get high. I knew this wasn't right, but at this time, I was full-blown addicted to cocaine and, honestly, had been for quite some time; I just didn't want to accept it. I no longer cared. I knew I liked getting high, and I had to do something to get it. I started proactively selling myself and tricking to get what I wanted—drugs! I no longer had any respect for myself or my body. Getting high felt sooooo good there was no room for respect. Inside, I wasn't happy with myself. I had low self-esteem. I didn't care about myself anymore. I just wanted to lay around doing nothing but getting high.

One summer day in 1988, Tiff and her family were going to North Carolina to her dad's mother's house, Grandmom Mildred, for their family reunion. Tiff asked me if I would like to go, and I said, "Yes, of course I would." That Friday came, and Tiff, her dad, her brother, and other family members, including myself, all loaded up in a van and two cars. We left around three in the morning to get a head start on the traffic. We got to Grandmom Mildred's house around 8:30 a.m., and she had breakfast cooked already for us. She made bacon, eggs, fried potatoes, grits, scrapple, sausage gravy and biscuits, and more. We were in our glory with all this good Southern cooking. I told Tiff, "I'll come visit your grandmom with you anytime." Tiff just started laughing and said, "I know you would."

After breakfast, we all had to go check in to our hotel rooms. Tiff and her uncle Ethan and I shared a room. Ethan had a thing for me, and I knew it. You see, Ethan smoked cocaine as well. He would smoke with us sometimes, but most of the time, he did his own thing. We only brought a little bit with us. I was okay with that. We needed a break from smoking coke anyway. Tiff left the room for a little while, and Ethan and I had sex. It didn't mean anything to me anyway. We were just messing around. It wasn't like I was in a relationship or anything at the time.

After everyone was settled into their rooms, we all had to meet back up at Grandmom Mildred's house to discuss the setup for the family reunion. While there, we decided to play some volleyball out in the yard. Everyone got together and picked teams. We had so much fun that afternoon. Later that evening, we played this drinking game. I can't remember the name of it. All I do remember is that we were all *drunk* by midnight, and that was when we went back to our hotel rooms for the night.

The next day, we all got up early to go back over Grandmom Mildred's for another round of her breakfast, something we were all happy to do. We loved her cooking. After breakfast, we all went back to our rooms to chill out for a bit, until it was time to go to the family reunion. The reunion was being held at the Mill Creek Park. Around 1:00 p.m., everyone loaded up in their vehicles, and we all headed to the park. Once we were there, it was *on and poppin'*. We played all kinds of games: volleyball, softball, basketball, and of course, line dancing.

We had hamburgers, hot dogs, chicken, ribs—I mean, there was so much food everywhere. We had such an awesome time. By evening, everyone was tired, full, and done for the evening. We loaded ourselves back in the cars and headed back to our hotel rooms for the night.

On Sunday, we all got up and started packing and cleaning up to get ready to hit the road to head back home to Delaware. As we pulled out, we stopped by Grandmom Mildred's to say goodbye to her and the rest of the family. Once we were back in our hometown, things went back to normal. Tiff and I hooked up with a couple of our drug dealer friends so we could get high.

A month had passed since the reunion, and I found out that I was pregnant by Ethan, Tiff's uncle. I was so upset and mad at myself. Ethan and I were just friends, nothing more. I had messed with him a couple of times before, but that one time, I didn't use a condom, and this was the result.

I told Ethan about the pregnancy, and he wanted me to keep it, but after talking to him about it, he understood why I didn't want to keep it. I was in no way ready to be a drug addict mom. I didn't want to bring a child into my mess. So he gave me the money to get the abortion. I was so broken and had mixed emotions, but I knew I was doing the right thing for me.

Chapter 5

Going Nowhere, Part II

During the summer of 1989, I met this guy named Morris. One night hanging out with my cousin Candy on the Strip, the name of a street that was a popular hangout in Dover, Delaware, for people that hung in the streets late night. He and his boy Brick were drug dealers, and I knew it. We talked for a little bit that night but soon went our separate ways. The next night, Candy and I went to this club called the Elks. It was a place Candy and I would go to once in a while to get our dance and our drink on. I ran into Morris again. He was standing outside of the club, talking to his boys. Morris was a nice-looking guy. He was about five eight or five nine, dark skinned, average build, with dimples and a pretty smile.

We exchanged numbers that night, and as the days passed, he and I would talk on the phone, taking our time to get to know each other. He told me he was just getting out of a relationship with someone, which worked for me because I wasn't looking for anything too serious. Therefore, I told him maybe we could just hang out sometime. He was cool with that.

A few days later, Morris called me and asked me if he could take me out to eat. I said sure. That evening he picked me up from my cousin's house, and we went to Wings to Go, one of my favorite places to eat. Morris and I started messing around and having sex after that "date." I knew what Morris was into. He was a drug dealer. That didn't bother me at all. Besides, I *really* started to fall hard for him. I told him I smoked cocaine, and he didn't like that at *all*! I wouldn't do it around him, nor would I talk about it around him. Eventually I moved in with Morris just a few months after we started talking. We lived together, and it was good for a minute, until I found out I was pregnant. When I told Morris, he asked me, "What do you want to do?" Again, confused and scared, I said to him, "I'm not ready to have a baby. *Look at me*, I'm stuck on cocaine and I'm scared." So he gave me the money to get an abortion. This was my second abortion in *one* year! I was so messed up in my head I beat myself up about having two abortions; I was mad, scared, tired, and lost! I didn't share how I was feeling with anyone, and for the first time in a long time, I was actually starting to wonder what kind of life I was heading toward.

The night of the abortion, I felt like I reached an all-time low. I was depressed and tired of getting high, but I didn't know how to fix it. I prayed that night that I would overdose and that all my pain would just be over. Unfortunately, this didn't happen. Instead, we moved on with our lives, and I never shared with anyone about my prayer. We continued to live together in his apartment in New Castle. I got a job at a small convenient store by the apartments, and I started to do a little better. I was no longer getting high every day, like I used to. Working helped to keep me busy. That way I wouldn't be thinking about getting high. I knew Morris wanted me to stop, and *I* wanted to stop. It's just that that drugs can really take you *there*. It was very *hard* to stop something that you really enjoyed doing, even though it was *bad*! I tried to do whatever I could to keep it hidden from Morris.

I started hooking back up with my girl Tiff, my bestie. She had moved in with her sister, Nish, in Wilmington. By now, you already know when Tiff and I get together, it's nothing nice. I was only working part-time at the store, but I had just gotten paid, so I had money to burn. I wanted to get high, so I told Tiff, "Let's go get some coke to smoke." We did just that, and there we were, off to the races. What made it worse was that once the money ran out, we would look for other means to get high. Most of the time that meant Tiff and I would go trick with someone to get more drugs. However, since I was in a relationship, I wasn't tricking at that time, so Tiff would go do her thing and bring us back more coke to smoke.

One day I was in our apartment, and I found one of the hiding spots where Morris would keep his money and his drugs. I started stealing his money and drugs—*that was probably one of worst things I could have done.* But again, I didn't care. I was hooked.

It was April 1990, and Morris and I had been together for about ten months, almost one year approaching in June, and I was in love with him. I was still trying to kick my drug habit, but it was not working. I found out I was pregnant again, but this time, I told Morris I wanted to keep my baby. This was my third pregnancy, and I was feeling really emotional about the situation. I knew I couldn't keep having abortions, and I really didn't *want* to have another one anyway. Also, at the time, I was feeling good about my relationship with Morris. Morris knew I was in love with him and that I wanted his child. But he already had three children, so he wasn't all that thrilled about having another one. I asked him, "Aren't we family? You tell me you love me and that you want to stay with me." We talked about our future together, and I was hoping we would get married one day and that I would be clean from drugs.

Well (sigh), I decided to keep my baby, and each day I struggled with smoking cocaine. Morris and I moved to Dover. We started staying at his mom's house temporarily until I had the baby. Tiff had moved back to her dad's house in the country. I would go over to Tiff's dad's house and smoke with them. I knew I was wrong, *and yes*, I worried about my unborn child all the time, asking God to help me. You don't understand. I had been smoking hard-core for about three years now, and it was not that easy to just *stop*! At this point, I didn't know how to stop.

There were days Morris would go looking for me to see if I was using drugs. He knew Tiff and I were best friends and that we got high together. He would show up at her dad's house unannounced to catch me and make me leave and go home. Morris wasn't wrong. He had every right to be mad at me and cuss me out. I just didn't know how to handle my addiction. Here I was, still going *nowhere*.

This went on the whole summer of 1990. I kept on smoking all while praying, asking God to allow me to have a healthy baby. Morris and I started to have problems in our relationship, and I knew we weren't going to last much longer.

January 19, 1991, I gave birth to my daughter, Leeah. She was seven pounds, sixteen ounces, healthy and beautiful. I had already moved out of Morris's mom's house a couple of months before I had our baby girl. I started staying with one of my girlfriends, Joy. I was very happy that she allowed me and my daughter to come and stay a couple of months until I could find somewhere for me and Leeah to live in. I became homeless.

March 1991, I moved into a thirty-day shelter. I then left there and moved in with my daughter's aunt Jean, who was Morris's sister-in-law. She and I had and still have a good relationship. She allowed me and Leeah to stay until I could figure out what to do next. I ended up applying for Section 8, low-income housing, and was just waiting until I could get approved. Meanwhile, Morris and I broke up, and he was sent to prison in June for selling drugs.

Through a conversation with Tiff, I then found out that there was a long-term shelter in Wilmington. So I called the YWCA in Wilmington, got all the information, and made an appointment to see if I could get housing with them. By the end of June 1991, Leeah and I moved into the shelter at the YWCA. I was very happy, I wasn't homeless, and I wasn't a burden to anyone anymore.

After getting settled into the shelter, I had a meeting with Ms. Brown, who was the manager of the house. She explained to me the rules and regulations of Home Life Management, the name of the shelter. I also had a curfew. We had to be in by 10:00 p.m. I met a few girls in the shelter. Everyone seemed nice, and being that I was a social butterfly, I loved being around people. I got along with everyone. One girl I met, Sarah was her name, had five children and was pregnant with her sixth. Jokingly I remember saying to her, "I don't know how you do it. I barely can take care of myself and Leeah."

Well, it didn't take long to find out that we both liked to get high smoking that cocaine. It just seemed like everyone was doing it. I felt like I couldn't get away from it!

Sarah and I became very good friends. We would watch each other's kids, well, her kids and my one (LOL). We started getting high together, which was not a good thing. The father of Sarah's children eventually found a place for them to live. Knowing how close Sarah and I had become, he offered for me to come and stay with them, until my Section 8 came through. He explained that it wasn't a lot of room, but we could make it work. I kindly accepted the offer. I stayed in the shelter from June 1991 to January 1992. Sarah and I both left the shelter and moved into her home. While staying with Sarah, we would steal her boyfriend's drugs, and whenever he would come to the house and bag it up, we would help him. We would sneak and take turns taking a hit of the coke, while the other kept a lookout for someone coming by. This became the norm for us almost every day.

Luckily, I only had to stay with her for a month and a half. I received my letter stating that my Section 8 was approved, and I could start looking for a place. I only had until that April to find a place to live, or my Section 8 would expire.

I found a place in Wilmington, a two-bedroom apartment, and moved into our new home in April 1992. At the same time, I found out I was pregnant again. I started messing around with this guy I met in January 1992, one of Sarah's friends. His name was Darren. He was actually staying in a halfway house when I met him and was about to be released from doing some time in jail. I didn't even know Darren that well, and here he was, the father to my unborn child. I didn't understand. We had only gotten together a couple of times during his weekend visits home. For the most part, we did use condoms, but once again, the one time I didn't was the time I got pregnant. I was *very* upset with myself for allowing myself to get pregnant again, knowing I was addicted to cocaine. I didn't want or need any more kids at that time, especially since I had my daughter that I could barely take care of. I decided I was going to get an abortion. I told his mom, whom I called Mom Pat. Mom Pat was a pastor, a woman of God, and very spiritual. One day, after talking to her about my plans, she, along with one of her Evangelist girlfriends, came over and prophesied over my stomach. They prayed over me and the baby, pleading for me not to abort this child. They told me God had a special plan for the child and for me to keep my baby. Well, after hearing that, I couldn't go through with the abortion. I decided to keep my baby, and I'm so glad I did. I found out later through an ultrasound that I was going to have a *boy*!

As my daughter and I got situated in my new apartment, I would allow Darren to stay over sometimes. Darren and I didn't get along that well. You see, he smoked cocaine too. This became a big problem for us. It was bad enough I was smoking the whole time of my pregnancy. I was putting my unborn son at risk of becoming a drug-addicted baby. I really wanted to stop not only for myself but, more importantly, for the sake of my baby. Unfortunately, I couldn't control the drug; the drug was controlling me. I was so weak, unloved, passive, naive and just plain ignorant to it all. Having Darren around only made my situation worse. I was never his girlfriend. We just liked each other and messed around. At least I thought he just liked me, but Darren became obsessed with me.

I gave birth to my son in December 1992. He was so small because of my drug use and smoking cigarettes. He weighed only five pounds, six ounces. He was considered low birth rate. Because he was born with withdrawals and there was cocaine in my system, the hospital notified child protective services. I was so happy he wasn't deformed, but he did have a few withdrawals from the drug. Overall though, he was healthy. I named him Devin. For about a year following my son's birth, I had Social Services on my back. They would perform home visits and would send a nurse every couple of months to visit Devin to make sure he was growing and developing correctly. They had to make sure he was healthy and had no lasting complications. He was later diagnosed with ADHD.

One day in March 1993—Devin was three months old, and Leeah, fourteen months old—I had the kids in their bedroom taking a nap. I was sitting home, chilling, worn-out because I had just gotten back home from visiting some cousins in Cecilton, Maryland. I had left on a Friday and came back the next day, one day earlier than when I was supposed to. In the complex I lived in, I had a neighbor, Mr. Black, who used to check me out and try and get with me. He was married, and I wasn't into messing around with married men. We used to sit on our porches and talk in general, nothing serious. He always just flirted with me. As I lay on the couch, all I could think about was the fact that I didn't have any money, and I needed to get high—this monkey (devil) was always on my back. I remembered how Mr. Black would always tell me if I let him go down on me, he'd pay me. I always told him no, but on this one particular day, he was going to get his wish. I decided to take Mr. Black up on his offer. I told Mr. Black that he could come over and "handle business" for some money. Surprised at my offer, he immediately came over to my place, and we went into the bedroom. As I lay on the bed, and Mr. Black started to do his business on me, all of a *sudden*, Darren comes flying out of my hallway closet, *screaming*, "I'm going to *kill you*, b———!" I was in total shock! I started screaming and jumped up, trying to pull my pants up, while Mr. Black pulled out a small knife and said to him, "If you go near her, I will stab you," *and he was dead serious*. I ran out the front door and ran out across the street to call 911 on the pay phone. I didn't have a house phone at this time. I then ran into the corner Chinese store, screaming and crying, asking the lady to call the police. She kept yelling for me to get out, but I told her, "*No*, not until you call the police … Someone was after me." Meanwhile, Darren had run out the back door of my apartment and went across the street but did not come into the store where I was. He saw me through the door.

    I came to find out this crazy fool left the window unlocked in my back bedroom and broke into my apartment while I was in Maryland staying with my cousins. When I came back one day earlier, he decided to hide in my hallway closet. I had no idea he was in there. *Who does that!* This nut never came out to use the bathroom, eat, nothing—unbelievable.

    At the end of April 1993, I moved from Wilmington to the suburbs in Bear, Delaware, a development called Brookmont Farms. I wanted to raise my kids out of the city. Mom Pat told me about this place since she also was in the process of moving there herself. This was a good thing, because I wasn't familiar with the area, but she knew it well. She would also watch the kids for me, when needed.

She actually moved one street over from me. I could walk out of my house and go through my backyard and be at her house. Now at this point, I liked my townhouse. It wasn't an apartment and was really nice. Being social, I started making new friends in the neighborhood pretty quickly.

After that incident with Darren, he and I hadn't talked in a few weeks. One day he was over his mom's house, and he asked his mom if she would let Devin come over so that he could see him. Mom Pat came over and took Devin to her place for a visit.

Crazy enough, I did get high a few more times with Darren, knowing I should not have. He wasn't stable. But one day I finally told him that all I wanted to do was raise our son with his help and that was it.

Once I was settled in my new home, Candy started to come over again, and of course, we got high. We met a few people out there, so it didn't take long to find out who was dealing and who was getting high. Of the people we met, we became friends with Dot and Cherry. They were a couple of girls that lived out there. They got high as well. Go figure, no matter where I moved to, the drugs always seemed to find me.

Living close to Mom Pat gave me great relief. She was a trusted person who knew all about my struggle with cocaine and knew I was actively getting high. As a matter fact, she knew her son and Candy got high as well. She would pray for me and Candy every day to get our lives back on track and together. I started calling her my spiritual mom! She became someone I could talk to about myself and the pressure of being on drugs. I would cry to her and tell her that I wanted to stop! I would tell her how tired I was, but I didn't know how to stop. She told me to *pray* and ask God to take it away from me every day. She told me to talk to God and build a relationship with him. She also told me to read Psalms 23 and Psalms 91 and to keep reading them. Mom Pat taught me how to pray and seek Jesus Christ!

As the summer approached, Candy would stay over from time to time. We would sit outside in the backyard, talk, and throw hot dogs and burgers on the grill for us and the kids. As we spent more time outside, I started to notice one of the guys that lived another street over from where I lived. It just so happened that one day, while Candy and I were out back, he was walking through this path on the side of my house (there was a lot of foot traffic there; people often used it as a shortcut to get to the other side of the neighborhood quicker). He stopped in my yard and introduced himself as TW.

As time went by, TW started stopping by my house to sell me some coke. He seemed to be a decent guy but another drug dealer. He was a little taller than I was, light skinned, hazel eyes, and goldish-colored hair. The more he came around, the more I found myself becoming more and more attracted to him. However, he had a girlfriend, one daughter, and two sons, and at that time, he was living with one of his sons' mom's, just a couple of streets over from me.

Because we were spending so much time around each other, the feelings I had for him became mutual. TW and I started having sex and messing around here and there. Even though I knew he had a girl, I fell hard for him, and I couldn't shake him off that whole summer. I knew I was just the side chick, and I was okay with that. Besides, I was still tricking with other drug dealers around the area. Around this same time, I met this older guy named Dan. He was a dealer that I met at a friend's house in the same development. He was about six one, bald in the middle of his head, with patches of hair on each side, and had big eyes with glasses. He thought he was *all* that because he sold cocaine. Well, he ended becoming one of his own best customers, breaking the number 1 law of dealerhood: *Never get high on your own supply*. His world was about to be turned upside down.

Unfortunately, Dan started to smoke coke too, and it was all downhill after that. He and I would smoke together all the time. He would either come to my house, or we would meet at a mutual friend's house. Dan and I were never intimate. I never really liked him like that. He wanted to, but every time he would get high, his penis would be lame; therefore I would play him and say, "Yeah sure, after we get high," knowing he couldn't get hard (LOL).

One particular night, Dan and I were at my house, upstairs in my bedroom getting really high, smoking the night away. It was in the middle of August 1993, on a hot summer night, and I had my windows opened. I was lying on the floor, and Dan was sitting on the floor leaned up against the footboard of my bed. It was around 10:00 p.m., and we were just getting high—no sex. While we sat there talking, I suddenly heard this voice say, "Are you having fun?" I knew I was high, but I wasn't sure if I was hearing things. I looked around but decided it was nothing, so I continued to lay there, and I heard it again: "Are you having fun?" I look over at Dan, and I said, "Did you hear that?" Dan looked at me with his big wide eyes and said, "No! I didn't hear anything," looking at me as if I was hearing things or losing my mind. Next thing you know, I heard it again, "Are you having fun?" I looked at Dan, and he said, "I heard it that time." As soon as he said that, my son's dad, Darren, came flying through my window, busting the screen and landing on my floor, yelling, "I'm going to *kill* you, b——!" I jumped up superfast and started running toward the stairs, screaming, "He's going to kill me!" Still yelling, Darren was running behind me, and Dan was running behind Darren—both of us scared to death.

My cousin Candy was downstairs watching a movie with our neighbor, Chase. Chase jumped up and said "What the hell" as I flew past him and ran to the back room of my house, into my kids' room to hide. He stopped Darren from chasing after me and opened up the front door and pushed him outside while telling him, "Man, I will kill you if you try and come back in this house." Meanwhile, Dan was standing at the bottom of the stairs, scared, and my cousin was beyond confused. She just kept asking, "What just happened?" Outside, Darren started banging on the side of the house, still screaming, "I'm going to kill you!" I just knew this time, he was going to hurt me. I was so scared.

Candy came into my kids' room to rescue me, and we both just looked at each other in shock. Candy said, "I can't believe it. Darren has lost his mind." That night I became really scared, very paranoid to be home, especially with him nearby. I was starting to think that he really wanted to kill me. Especially since I had to call the cops on him at least twice before.

The next day, Candy and I woke up and still couldn't believe what had transpired that night before. We talked about it, and I decided to really leave Darren alone. I realized his obsession for me was unpredictable and unnerving. I told Mom Pat what happened, and she couldn't believe his actions. She said to me, "You know it's the drugs," and I told her, "I know, but not all of it is the drugs." After that, I cut my son's father out of my life.

Candy decided to stay with me, to help me with the kids and to help me feel safer. I was grateful for her being there, especially since it was just me and my kids that lived there anyway. Following that event, I continued to get high and mess around with different guys. Some were dealers, and some were just regular old men that I would meet through mutual friends. We called them Sugar Daddies. Most of the time I could manipulate them out of some money without having to do anything for it. I used them to my advantage to get what I wanted.

Not only did I use guys, but Candy and I would also go into department stores and steal clothes and then come back later, to customer service, to return the items. They would ask for the receipt, and if we didn't have it, they would ask for our IDs and give us a full refund. I was doing things I thought I would never do, my life had become dependent on this drug, I was addicted, and I didn't know how to stop. Things were becoming very scary for me.

By end of 1993, going into 1994, I decided to move back into the city. I wanted to get away from the neighborhood, and I wanted a fresh start, *again*. I wanted to try and get my life together.

Chapter 6

God, Help Me

In April 1994, I finally moved back into the city into an apartment on Washington Street, in Wilmington, Delaware. It wasn't a bad area, but it wasn't the greatest. It was okay for what we needed.

After a couple of months of adjusting to my new apartment, I came to know the young lady that lived downstairs, beneath me. Her name was Mel. Mel had two sons but got high as well. When I learned this fact, I said to myself, "How am I ever going to get clean if it's always around me?" Not only did Mel smoke, but my girlfriend Sarah from the shelter back in 1991 and another friend, Red, started hanging out at my apartment again. We would sit around, drinking and smoking just like the old days. It was déjà vu all over again.

As days were going by, I would reflect on how many people I met. Everyone seemed to be tied to this drug. They were either drug dealers, neighbors, drug users, or all the above. Every now and then I would pray and ask God to help me to stop getting high. I really didn't like myself anymore and was beginning to feel more and more worthless.

My home had become a revolving door, open to all kinds of people I didn't really know. I'd like to say that everyone I had coming through my home was a friend, but the reality was I barely knew who most of them were. The scariest part of all was that my children lived through the revolving faces too.

I began to slip further and further into despair. Unfortunately, life wasn't quite done with me. One morning, during the summer of

1994, I was awoken by a hard blow to the head. Foggy and confused, I struggled to open eyes wide enough to see what was happening, but before I could get my eyes focused, I was hit again upside my head. At this time, I began struggling to roll from under the weight that had me bound. As I did, I got a good view of the person on top of me. It was Darren! He had broken into my home and began beating me. In that moment, all I could think to do was run. I wrestled with him hard enough to where I managed to escape his fist and grips. I ran out of the room and down the stairs, and as I frantically opened the front door, it swung back and hit me in the face. Not only was I battered and bruised from Darren hitting me, I now had this huge gash above my eye. Because my adrenaline was pumping, the gash didn't slow me down. I don't recall if Darren followed me out of the house or not; all I remember is feeling if I didn't get out, he was going to kill me. I managed to make it to the corner store, with blood pouring down my face. I begged the owner to call the police. When they finally arrived, I explained what happened to the police and allowed the paramedics to stitch me up. When the police finally caught Darren, I eagerly pressed charges, especially since this was not the first time he had laid hands on me. Later I learned that Darren's motive for his sneak attack was because I wouldn't deal with him after his last attack.

    Shortly after that ordeal, I met this guy. His name was Thomas, but they called him T-Bone. I met T-Bone through my downstairs neighbor, because they would smoke cocaine together. T-Bone was tall, about six one, dark skinned, with pretty dark eyes and a beautiful smile. Not to mention, his body. *Wow*, he was muscular, built and fine! T-Bone and I hit it off fairly quickly. It wasn't long till he started to come over my apartment and get high with me sometimes—of course, only if I was there by myself.

    In between the times T-Bone and I were not together, I would be getting high with different people. Things started to get really bad for me, and depression began to really sink in. I no longer loved myself, but whenever T-Bone came around, I instantly began to feel better about myself. He made me feel like I had a life worth living. He and I would have serious talks about our future and what we wanted. I told him I wanted to stop getting high. He also wanted the same. We did not realize the stronghold it had on our lives until we started to see it. T-Bone and I became official during the summer of 1994. I fell head over heels over that man.

Although we both wanted to stop getting high together, we began scheming up various ways to continue to get high. T-Bone started making fake cocaine to sell so that we could get money and go buy the real coke. We were starting to live dangerously.

In the midst of my crazy, dangerous life, tragedy happened in my family. In May of 1995, one Saturday morning, we were getting dressed to go to my cousin Nevy's wedding in Cecilton, Maryland, and I called my grandfather to see what time he was going to pick me up. On that phone call, he told me that there had been a terrible car accident involving my cousin Nellie; her sister, Steffy; and Nellie's children, Coco and Veno. Coco was killed instantly (she was only four years old). My grandfather came and picked me and my kids up and took us over to cousin Nevy's house to meet up with the rest of the family.

Nellie was listed in critical condition at Union Hospital in Maryland. Veno and Steffy had a few bruises and scratches but were okayed to go home. My entire family gathered together in prayer for Nellie's recovery. She passed away a week later. This hit me to my core, and I felt like a ton of bricks landed on top of me. I couldn't move. All I could do was cry. Nellie and all my cousins and I were all around the same age and were very close. Growing up, we were like sisters and brothers. I recall that night, after my grandfather dropped me and the kids off back home, all I could do was cry myself to sleep. I didn't even think about getting high.

About two weeks after my cousin's passing, I found myself still trying to get it together and over her death. At that time, Leeah was four years old, and Devin was about 2.5 years old. Not to mention, on top of the recent death, I was told I needed to move out of my place in May.

Luckily, I only moved a couple blocks away, onto Jefferson Street. This area was much quieter than my previous location. T-Bone moved in with me, and I even stopped tricking with other guys and dealers in respect of our relationship. T-Bone started providing our drug needs by primarily making his fake drugs and selling them. I would plead with him to stop doing it because it was too dangerous. I knew firsthand how desperate people are when they need their high and the things people would do. All I could think about was that someone was going to hurt him. He wouldn't listen to me though, but he did compromise with me. We decided to use my welfare check and sell food stamps to get high; therefore, only when we didn't have any money would he go do that nonsense. I was still uncomfortable with it, but I wasn't going to push too hard for him to stop.

T-Bone was always on the hustle for drugs. One night in August, he brought home this black handgun. I hated guns, and he knew this. He was so eager to show it to me I figured he wasn't using it for protection. I asked him, "What are you going to do with that?" Excitedly he said, "I'm going go and try to sell it, babe. We should get a good couple dollars for this." Instantly, I knew this was going to be trouble. Later that evening, T-Bone asked me to walk with him on the streets to see if we could find a buyer. We headed down to Price's Park, near Jessup Street. It was warm out, so people were hanging out everywhere. T-Bone saw this Jamaican drug dealer from New York he had bought from before. He walked over to the Jamaican and made some small talk with him initially, but then he leaned in to tell him about the gun. T-Bone told the guy that it was a .9 mm, and he wanted to sell it. Leery of the entire situation, I kept my distance and stood about ten to fifteen feet away from them. Now, I've been in some scary situations, but for some reason, I had terrible knots in my stomach about this gun. Something just wasn't sitting right within me.

The gun was loaded when T-Bone handed it over to him, so the guy held the gun and tried to cock it back, but it kept jamming. At that moment, the police rode by, and I became increasingly paranoid. I started motioning for T-Bone to come on, but he just kept saying, "Wait a minute." He told the guy, "It was just working before I came to you."

The guy tried again, and the gun was still jamming. The dealer got tired of trying to fool with that gun and gave it back to T-Bone, complaining, "I don't want it, it doesn't even work."

T-Bone took the gun and said "Okay, man," and we walked off.

When we got a little farther down the street, I looked at T-Bone, and I said, "There's a reason why that gun jammed." I told him, "I kept getting a bad feeling, as if the dude was going to shoot us and not give you nothing for the gun. To be honest, babe, I think God had his angels with us the whole time."

T-Bone said, "Yeah, you're probably right, because the gun worked fine earlier."

As we walked back home, I reflected on what just happened. I could have been shot and killed, and my babies wouldn't have a mom anymore. It freaked me out!

As the winter months started approaching, I found myself praying a little more. I would ask God to help me. I was getting really tired of getting high, and I wanted to quit, but I was scared and lost.

Sometime in December 1995, around Christmas, T-Bone and I went to the department store to do some Christmas shopping for my kids. T-Bone didn't have any children, but he was a good stepdad to my kids. He loved my babies. We bought all kinds of toys and clothes and things. Christmas was always important to me. However, about a week before Christmas, T-Bone had sold most of the kids' Christmas gifts to buy coke. I was so hurt and mad at the same time. I couldn't believe he did that to my babies. I just cried and kept asking him why, and just like most addicts, he felt really bad after the fact. I didn't have any more money to buy them anything else. Reality sat in, and I said to him with nothing but sincerity in my heart, "We both need to get our lives together and get help." Because I knew it was the addiction and not the person, I stayed with T-Bone after that situation. I loved that man, and I really wanted us to work out.

CHAPTER 7

Delivered and Free—Only God

In January of 1996, T-Bone and I had been together now for about seven months, and I didn't want to be with anyone else but him.

That month was extra special that year because my girlfriend Sarah, who already had six children, was pregnant by my younger brother, Jay, with her seventh child. It was January 7, 1996, and we were in the midst of a winter storm. Sarah was at her mom's house when she started to have contractions. They had to call the ambulance to come get her, and by that night, my niece was born—my first niece. I was so happy for Sarah and my brother (even though they were not together anymore).

T-Bone and I couldn't wait until Sarah came home from the hospital to celebrate. Of course, our celebration was to get high. A few days passed by, and Sarah went home to her mom's house first but then came over to my house to stay a couple of days. All three of us got high and kept getting high for days. I was so tired.

T-Bone was still going out, selling his fake drugs, causing us to get into big arguments because I wanted him to stop doing it. I would cry to him, saying, "I don't want to see anything happen to you. You could end up hurt or dead." The drug always seemed to win us over. I knew I wanted to stop, and I was trying to figure out how to do it.

In March of 1996, my birthday was approaching on the seventeenth, and I was getting ready to turn twenty-nine. All I could think about was how I had been smoking cocaine for nine years. I could not believe that I had been using drugs that long. I was so disgusted with myself. I wanted to change. I wanted to get my life back. I remember T-Bone asking me what I wanted to do for my birthday. In my mind, I wanted to do something different, but it was like I was stuck in a twilight zone and couldn't get out. Of course, my birthday came, and T-Bone, Sarah, Red, and I got high.

As fate would have it, a few days later, T-Bone got arrested for violation of probation. I was devastated and didn't know what to do. I was used to him being there with me and for me. I went to see his mom, and she allowed me to come into her home so that I could talk to him on the phone when he called her (I didn't have a phone). He told me that he would have to do about one year in prison. I was so upset I just cried and cried. I started making appointments to go visit him at least once a week, and so I wouldn't feel totally alone, I would ask Sarah to come and stay some nights.

I was still getting high with friends and associates, but not as often as I was before. One day when I went to visit T-Bone, I told him I really wanted to stop getting high. I told him I was tired, and I wanted better for myself and my kids. He said, "Well, you're going to have to try real hard and stop letting people come over to get high. Since people need a place to get high, you're going to stop them from coming over to use your house."

I said to him, "Yeah, easier said than done."

In his most supportive way, he said, "I know, but you will have to try."

That following July, I was home, chilling, not doing much, kind of bored in fact. This particular day was one of those excruciatingly hot days, those days where you just didn't have the energy to do anything at all. I didn't have an air conditioner in the apartment, so I would have the kids take two to three showers a day to stay cool. Later on that night, I decided to buy some coke and get high by myself. Now, usually I didn't get high by myself in the past. I had only done that once or twice. But this particular night, I decided to do it. I put the kids to bed, turned on my music, and I started to get high. After only hitting the pipe two or three times, my heart started beating really fast. In my nine years of using, this had never happened before. Instantly I became scared. I looked down at my chest, and all I could see was my heart bulging out from my chest as if it was going to *burst*. I ran to the bathroom and flushed the cocaine down the toilet and threw the pipe away. In my panic, I kept crying out, "God, please help me!" I just knew I was getting ready to go into cardiac arrest. I cried out, "Oh God, please don't let me die!" Just then a voice said, "Grab your Bible and read Psalms 23 and Psalms 91." Without hesitation, I grabbed my Bible (which I never kept too far away from me) and started off reading 23 followed with 91. I was pacing back and forth, reading those scriptures over and over again. As I walked and read, my heart would slow down a little bit, but as soon as I sat down, it would bulge from my chest and start racing. I was freaking out, but I kept reading, and I wouldn't stop. All I could think about was my kids waking up in the morning finding me *dead*! As I kept reading Psalms 23 and 91, I asked God to please not let me die. Desperate for help, I went outside and started pacing up and down the sidewalk, talking and praying to God. A male friend of mine that I would get high with sometimes stopped by while I was walking, and he asked me what I was doing out there. I told him what was going on, and he got spooked and walked off. He said, "If you die, I don't want to be here." I continued to pray and read Psalms 23 and 91 until my heart started beating regularly. By that time, it was around three in the morning. Once I started feeling better, I was exhausted and just wanted to go to sleep, but I was too scared to close my eyes. I was afraid I was not going to open them back up again.

Apparently, I did fall asleep, because when I woke up later that morning, I had my Bible lying on top of my chest. When I realized that I was okay, I jumped up and just began giving God a tearful praise of gratitude. I kept yelling, "I'm alive! I'm still here!" All I could do was thank God so much for *saving me*!

Right then and there, I promised God that I would serve him for the rest of my life for saving me. I was delivered and free, and it was only God who saved me!

I now have twenty-two years clean from crack cocaine. All glory goes to God!

About the Author

Shawnetta Brown resides in Delaware with her husband and beloved family. In her spare time, she enjoys serving at her local church, cooking for family and friends, and enjoying her everyday life!

CPSIA information can be obtained
at www.ICGtesting.com
Printed in the USA
LVHW090955240119
605105LV00001B/19/P